LITTLE PINK BOOK™

When Your Mom
Has Cancer

Helping Children Cope at Home and Beyond

Maryann Makekau

20/30north Studios

1

Copyright 2010, 2020 by Makekau
Graphic Design: 2030north Studios

For information, address:
Maryann Makekau
PO Box 2021
Fort Walton Beach, FL 32549

Set in Kristen ITC 12 point. Includes references.

A LITTLE PINK BOOK™ - When Your Mom Has Cancer: Helping Children Cope at Home and Beyond.
Library of Congress Cataloging (Pre-assigned Control Number)
Makekau, Maryann

ISBN-13: 978-0-9826601-6-4
ISBN-10: 0982660162

Note: The information in this book is true and complete to the best of our knowledge. This book is intended only as an informative guide for those wishing to know more about cancer issues. In no way is this book intended to replace, countermand or conflict with the advice given to you by your own physician. The ultimate decision concerning care should be made between you and your doctor. We strongly recommend you follow his or her advice. Information in this book is general and is offered with no guarantees on the part of the author or publisher. The author/publisher disclaims all liability in connection with use of this book.

 2

Foreword

One of the hardest trials in my life, besides losing a loved one, was experiencing the loss of naiveté through illness and the loss of health, and to realize that there are life experiences so out of our control. The diagnosis of cancer is such a scary one for all involved, equally so for myself as physician turned cancer patient. As women, we oftentimes have an unrecognized capacity for strength and courage. The basis of this is the love of our God and our family; with the realization that through Him we may not only endure, but be victorious in our journey through this life.

We are so used to being the loving caregivers in our family; that role reversal is often difficult. As loving, supporting, gentle givers, we must learn to instead be the fighter and the one to graciously accept assistance and love from others. One of the most important truths my oncologist, peer and friend, told me was that part of my role (as a friend and loved one) was to accept and even learn to ask for help. For many of us this is difficult but essential – not just for us enduring the fight, but for all those who love us. They cannot have surgery or take other treatments for us. In that, they can also feel helpless and frustrated. Instead, we can allow them to show their love by their words and deeds – and that is powerfully healing to us all.

The ones that most feel this burden are our spouses and children. It is very important for them to understand, in their own capacity, what is happening and what to expect. It is also comforting and strengthening to know that their actions and love are vital to our strength as women. Our children's sense of worth is key in their adjustment and healing during this stressful time during such formative years. Always reassure them when Mommy is not feeling well – that you are fighting the illness and expect to feel better soon. They will need encouragement and reassurance even long after the fight is won. Maryann's suggestions in this book regarding family time and prayers reinforce the power and hope these combined actions bring.

3

Through all this — hope, faith, love and humor are your best weapons. Always be willing to laugh at yourself. It can put you and others at ease. Laughter truly is a medicine that cannot be reproduced pharmaceutically.

Always remember that we are more than the sum of our appearance and shifting moods. At times in this journey, we may not always recognize ourselves in the mirror — but at the resolution we will emerge as our true beautiful selves. With the love of God and our family and friends, we may very well possess a more beautiful soul and purpose than we started with.

Maryann has done an amazing job at getting in the mindset of a child, and anticipating their questions and concerns from that unique perspective. As an adult, and as one who regularly speaks to and educates adults about breast cancer, I recognize we often take some of our knowledge-base for granted. We forget children are coming at this problem with not only a skewed sense of "illness," but also with a much cleaner slate.

The word cancer embodies so many fearful and disheartening ideas to adults, yet it has not been given a definition or form to most children. In some ways, this can be advantageous. The fast pro-gressing world of research and medicine has brought us treatments and improved outcomes not previously seen. We as adults have preset ideas and reactions to the word cancer, based on informa-tion that may be from 20 or 30 years ago. Our children's experi-ences are going to be different. During these changes and advances, we have the ability to teach and form their perception of cancer. I hope these advances continue in an exponential fashion, so that in the future children will not experience such fear with a cancer diagnosis. Wouldn't it be amazing if those children helped to erase the disease from the future of mankind? The first key is to help with healthy understanding and the teaching of compassion.

L. Rebecca Baskin MD
Breast Surgeon
Comprehensive Breast Center at Murfreesboro Medical Clinic
www.mccbreastcenter.com

4

Gratitude

This Little Pink Book™ is dedicated to mothers and children who must journey through cancer – fighting the fight together. When cancer enters a home, children look to the adults in their life to help them understand and cope with the turmoil it brings. When mom is the one diagnosed, it presents special challenges for her: facing cancer head-on while simultaneously bringing comfort to those she loves. When Your Mom Has Cancer is dedicated to mothers diagnosed with breast cancer – seeking to bring hope, love and comfort during a most difficult time.

This book is dedicated to every mother who shared her journey with me in the course of writing this Little Pink Book.™ Special thanks to Tina, who shared her personal story and insight of cancer treatment. To Vicki for your belief in me to do this work and for helping me to touch lives through your journey. To Star, thank you for sharing your experience with breast cancer and your Angel's Touch massage therapy; your healing hands are a special gift.

To Loren, thanks for the child-like wonder that you share with me! To Ashley for sharing your young heart and your questions with me; your compassion is a special blessing. Thank you, Chuck for your steadiness on this journey of blessing others with Pink hope.

To Derek, my illustrator and graphic artist at 20/30north Studios, thank you for sharing your inspiration, enthusiasm and love for this series. Every stick-character radiates hope thanks to your amazing talent. To my friends and family for your prayers, love, support, and tireless reviews; you are my fuel.

5

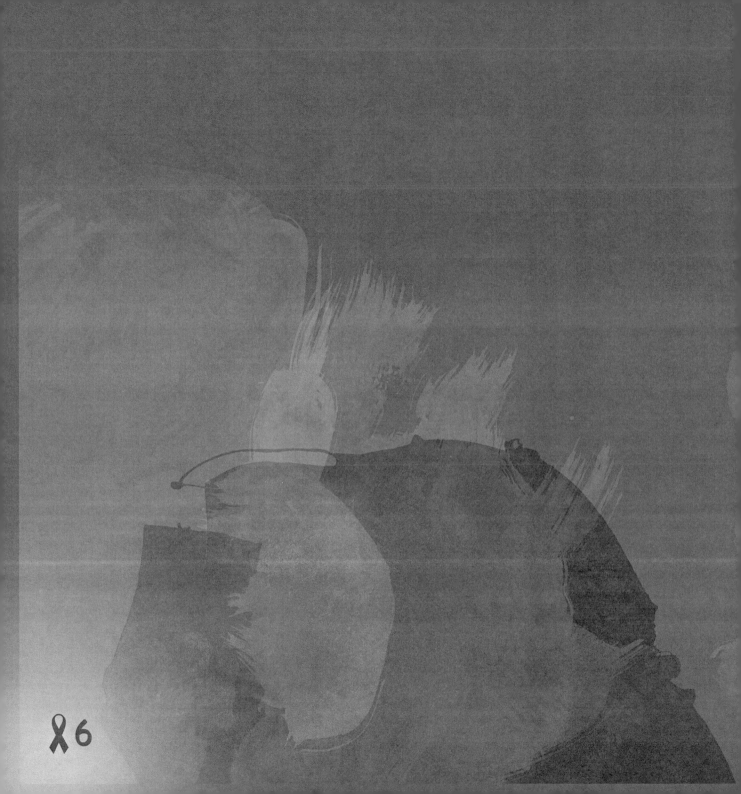

Table of Contents

Can You See Cancer?

Cancer is sort of odd because you might hear that someone has it, but you can't always see it – especially when it's on the inside! It can be inside the body in places like the breast, lungs, liver, stomach, or even in the brain. People with cancer know they have it because the doctor's tests show it.

That can all be very confusing, and you might wonder: if I can't see it, is it really there? You can see some parts of your body like your legs, arms, hands, feet and head. But there are other parts on the inside of your body that you can't see, like your brain, lungs, stomach and liver. You can't see them, but you know they're there because your brain helps you think and learn, your lungs help you breathe, your stomach helps you digest your food and your liver helps you get rid of things that are not healthy for your body (digest means to use up - then you're hungry again).

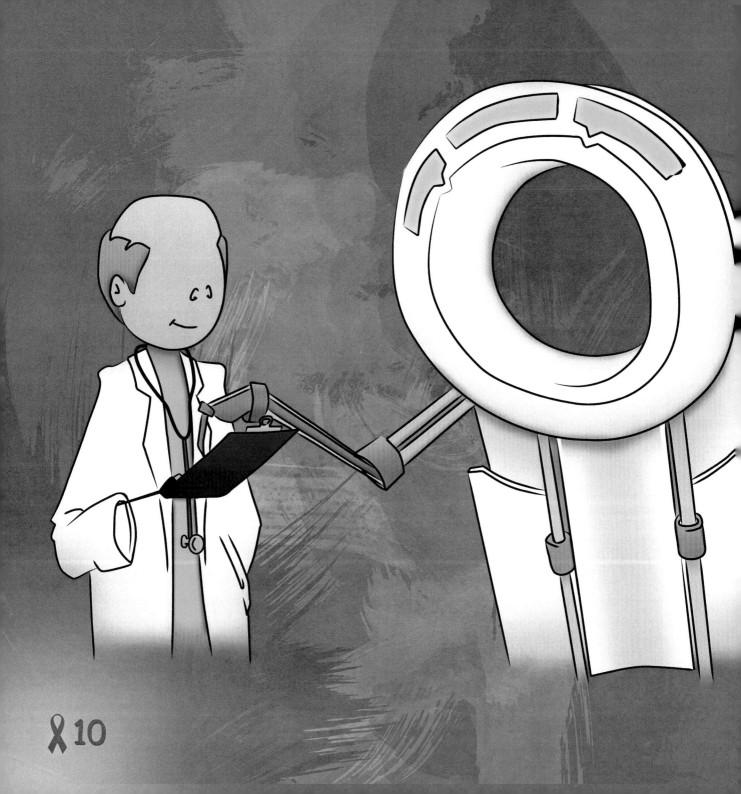

Since you can do all those things – think, breathe, eat and need to eat some more – you know all those parts are inside you, even though you can't see them!

So, even though you might not see cancer, doctors can see it. Doctors use special machines to see inside the body. Those machines can take pictures to see your bones and your brain, to see inside your lungs and even see inside your stomach. It's like the machines have super-powers that let doctors see through your skin! Doctors can sometimes even see cancer using those machines. They can see the places that cancer has hurt and the places it hasn't hurt.

There are different kinds of cancer and different ways to treat those cancers. And if doctors find the cancer early enough, it doesn't hurt the rest of the body.

11

Doctors try their best to help in healing the part of the body where the cancer is, no matter what kind of cancer it is. This book is about moms with breast cancer.

When someone you love has cancer, you may hear a lot of big words that you don't understand. Your mom may use some of them when she talks to friends and family. It's okay to ask your mom what those new words mean. You might be able to look them up together on the Internet. You might look in a "medical" dictionary at the doctor's office or at a bookstore. You might not remember them all, but it sure is fun to say such big words! Learning new words can help you ask really important questions too!

13

14

Talking About It

Cancer is something families should talk about. Have you ever had to wait your turn to talk at school? You raise your hand, and it can seem like forever before the teacher calls on you! Having something really important to say can make you feel anxious or worried. Sometimes we have to wait to share those really important things, but they should still be shared. Cancer is definitely something to talk about; even though it can be really hard to share, it should never be kept secret.

Secrets are for things like birthdays – like when you buy your mom a present and keep it a secret until it's time for the birthday party. Or when you help plan a "surprise party" for your grandma and you can't let her know before the party starts! Talking about things together means you trust each other!

15

Talking about things also makes you worry less. When you worry less, you have more energy for the really important stuff – like helping and playing! Everyone in your family should talk about cancer because it will make them worry less and feel better. Sharing your thoughts and feelings helps build trust.

Cancer won't go away just because you don't talk about it. And it won't get worse if you do talk about it! It can be really hard to talk about though. Sometimes people might get nervous or sad about it, and they might even cry.

It's very important to remember that it isn't anyone's fault that your mom has cancer. When you first find out that she has cancer you might wish that you could take it away somehow, make it disappear! You can't do anything "magical" to make it go away, but you can pray for your mom. You can even pray together as a family.

17

Does Cancer Hurt?

You might wonder if cancer hurts. Does it hurt like when you fall down and get a nasty bruise that turns black-and-blue? Does it hurt like when you break a bone? Does it hurt like when you get the flu and throw up a lot?

Cancer does hurt. It hurts when the person with it has to have surgery to remove the cancer. If your mom needs surgery to remove breast cancer, it will make her very, very sore for awhile!

Cancer hurts when medications called radiation and chemo-therapy cause "side effects." Side effects are bad things that happen to someone taking those medications. Even medications that help people sometimes cause side effects. Maybe you remember taking a medicine for a cold or cough that made you sleepy. That's a side effect, too.

Some side effects go away immediately while others take longer to go away. People who take medications for cancer might feel like throwing up and say that foods taste funny or have a hard time eating. Their head might hurt as they lose their hair – these are all "side effects." So, the answer is YES, cancer does hurt. But sometimes that hurt is part of getting better.

19

Cancer can hurt in other ways too. Cancer might cause people in your family to be afraid, cry or not sleep well. Remember, even though you can't see what's on the inside, it's still there, and it can still hurt! Worrying and not sleeping makes it hard to do your work at school. Adults might have trouble like that at their work too. But if your family asks questions and talks about cancer, everyone will worry less and sleep better.

It's even okay to ask your mom tough questions like "are you going to die?" It's normal to think about things like that when someone you love is hurting or gets very sick. It's okay to get answers to all your questions, so don't be afraid to ask, no matter what you're thinking.

Your mom will like it when you work hard in school and do your chores. But you still need to make time to laugh and have fun! Laughter is really, really good medicine and your happy face shows that you like sharing it!

Everyday Hugs

When someone has surgery and treatment for cancer, especially breast cancer, hugging might hurt too. You can save up your hugs, or there are some new ways to hug that you might want to know about!

Remember when you were really little and you would hug mom's legs or squeeze her waist? Of course, whether you hugged her legs or waist depended on how tall you were at the time!

It won't hurt your mom to hug her just like you used to when you were little – squeezing her waist or hugging her legs! Just make sure you don't hug her legs too tight – you don't want her to fall over!

You can also give shoulder hugs. Just sit next to her on the couch and get real, real close so that your shoulder is right against your mom's arm – that's called a "shoulder hug."

You can also give your mom a "lap hug." Kids like to sit in their mom's lap. Moms read stories from their lap and it's

 22

even a wonderful place to snuggle. Even big kids like to sit in their mom's lap sometimes! It's such a cozy feeling to be in mom's lap, even when you're too big to fit!

When a mom needs surgery for cancer it might hurt just to share her lap. But you can still give her a lap-hug. Just lay your head there instead of your whole body to get that same cozy feeling!

Why Do I Feel That?

Feelings can be really funny because there are so many different kinds, especially when someone you love is sick. And in families not everyone feels the same feeling at the same

happy   sad   angry

time! You may feel happy or sad. Your mom may feel bad or afraid. Sisters may feel confused or frustrated. Dads might get really mad or cry sometimes. Anyone in your family may feel all of those things at different times.

If you've ever moved to a new place or lost a pet, you understand some of those feelings. All of those feelings are okay.
Some days your whole family may be sad or cry.

scared   frustrated   confused

Cancer can be scary, especially when your mom can't do the
things she used to do everyday. You can talk to your mom,
your dad, your grandma, your teacher or even a friend about
those feelings.

It can help sometimes for families to pray together, like before dinner. Sharing feelings and praying is just like talking and can help everyone feel stronger.

Things might seem really hard sometimes and you might even imagine that everything is just like it was before mom got cancer. Some people call that "wishful thinking." Like when people say "wish upon a star." Others call it "hope." You might call it "faith." Even though you can't make your mom's cancer go away, having hope and faith helps everyone to feel better. When your mom is having a really sleepy, feeling bad kind-of-day she'll be really thankful that you share your hope!

27

Mom is Like Sleeping Beauty

It can take awhile to get rid of the cancer, and your mom may have to stay in the hospital overnight, or even longer. She will make sure that you have another adult like your grandmother, dad, aunt, babysitter or an adult friend with you at home – to make sure all the important things you need are taken care of. Your mom will be home with you as much as she can.

It can be really weird to see your mom napping so much. Most moms are up and doing things before their kids are awake and up after their kids go to bed. So you might feel sad or afraid when you see your mom so tired. Remember though, that your mom's body heals faster when she rests a lot more; so if she's in bed before you that's okay. You can even lie down next to her if you miss her. Just bring your favorite book and a flashlight to quietly lie near her. It will make mom smile just to know you're there, without having to say a word.

She might even want you to read a story to her sometimes too.

Mom is So Pretty

Medications can change the way your mom looks and feels. Remember how medications can cause "side effects" like making your mom feel sick or causing her hair to fall out? If your mom loses her hair, it might fall out quickly or slowly and then she'll be bald. Bald means having "no hair," and sometimes people go bald – with or without cancer. People without cancer can get sick too, like when they have a cold or the flu. Anyone who is sick should stay home and rest, so they can get better even faster.

Not every mom with cancer goes bald though. It depends on the treatment or medicine she receives. If her hair does fall out, it can make her head feel very tender and she might say ouch or cry when she touches her head. Sometimes, it might hurt even without touching it because it's so sore.

By the way, you can't catch cancer or the side-effects that come from cancer medicines! Cancer isn't like having a cold because it's not catchy. You can't get cancer by sitting next to your mom and you won't lose your hair if your mom does.

Cancer surgery and going bald are big changes for your mom. Even though she looks different, she's still the same person. Wearing a wig (fake hair) or scarves can make you look different. When cancer changes the way your mom looks, she might think or say that she doesn't feel "pretty" anymore.

Share those new hugs you learned about often! Hug your mom, and let her know that "pretty" comes from the inside! Tell her that she's still a really pretty mom and that you love her A LOT!

31

Collective Effort

When your mom is sick, you might wish you could do more! Even though you can't make her cancer go away, you can still be really helpful. Even the small things you do will help you feel stronger. When everyone in the family helps out, "collective effort" happens. Collective effort makes being helpful even better; together families make being helpful an even bigger blessing. And that makes families very, very strong.

It's important to remember that you didn't do anything to cause your mom's cancer and that you can still do lots of helpful things for your mom. You can pray for her. You can set the table for dinner and help another adult cook dinner (if that's allowed). You can do your chores without being asked or volunteer to do new chores. You can work hard at school. It's helpful just to wash your hands often, and cover coughs and sneezes, doing so helps everyone stay healthier. With everyone's help collective effort can make a big difference for your mom, your family, your school and even in other places in the world. It's like everyone is connected to each other!

33

Mom's Hats

Moms are used to doing a lot of things, and cancer can change that. Your mom might be your nurse when you fall and get hurt. She might be your listener when you have an argument with a friend. She might be your detective when you lose something and need help finding it. She might be your chauffeur when you need a ride to a friend's birthday party. She might be your chef who cooks amazing macaroni and cheese.

Your mom may do a lot of those things, but getting cancer can make it hard for her to do them like she used to. Your mom may need to take a temporary break from being a nurse, listener, detective, chauffeur or chef. She'll need a break from working so she can use that energy to get well! It's okay to let others help for awhile, like neighbors, friends, aunts, uncles, grandparents or anyone else who wants to help your family. That kind of collective effort makes an excellent gift for your mom while she's going through cancer.

Sharing Pink Hope

When people come together to make a difference, it can be extra pretty in pink. Did you know that people diagnosed with breast cancer and their families and friends often wear pink? They wear pink ribbons, pink bracelets, pink hats, pink shirts and they might even go to special events about cancer, like walks or races. That's sharing Pink hope!

There are many ways to help your mom and your family. Not sure what to do? Just ask your mom, dad, grandma, or anyone who's helping at your house! Ask your teacher at school! Hug others often, say "I love you" and fight the fight together!!!

36

37

PRE-TREATMENT TIPS FOR MOMS

1. Don't expect more of yourself than you can handle, even if it is different than yesterday or the day before.

2. Carefully weigh treatment options – medicines, surgery, traditional or non-traditional treatment, etc. Then do what is best for your unique self; ultimately, do what brings you serenity in the journey through cancer.

3. Remember to engage in something funny everyday. Look through old cards, notes and drawings you've saved from your children. Look through photo albums and watch funny movies. These are all pick-me-ups! Humor is one of God's best healing gifts.

4. Start hugging others until they let go – it's fun to see how long a hug lasts. This will be your storehouse during the times that hugging (the usual way) hurts. Get plenty of waist, leg, shoulder and lap hugs too!

5. Have a portable timer at your bedside or favorite chair. Let family and friends know that you're limiting visits so you won't overdo it. This is especially helpful with children; it will help them understand your need for rest and their need to do other things, besides spending time next to mom.

6. Consider your children's needs, for the usual and unusual days. Before treatment begins, try to arrange for help with the house (see "Cleaning for a Reason" - references below), grocery shopping and taking kids to school or taking them to after-school activities. For the unusual days, consider getting a medical power of attorney. Then in the event your child

gets sick or injured, someone else (a child care provider, trusted neighbor or relative) can manage a visit to the doctor or hospital. This could be especially important for single moms or moms whose husbands often work out of town.

7. Allow time to grieve; allow yourself to cry. Set a timer for 15 minutes and cry your eyes out – then clean up and move forward. Do this as often as necessary.

8. It's okay to get angry; it's a normal part of grief and God can take it! (p.s. Your family may need warning.)

9. Write down the things that you love about being a mom. Also list the things that make your kids unique in their own way. These lists will remind you of some really important reasons to rest and get well. They will help you to fight the fight even on the toughest of days!

10. Check-out for a short time each day. Pray and envision God's great big arms around you, taking away your fears one by one.

11. Look forward to a family "silly night." Between treatments (on a good day) wear silly hats and silly socks that don't match. Watch silly movies together and laugh till you cry! Tears express sadness, but they can also express sheer joy!

12. Find one thing you absolutely love about yourself and write it on a sticky note. Put this where you will see it often so when you look different, in the midst of the battle, you can meditate on what makes you lovely and special!

RESOURCES FOR MOMS AND KIDS

Helpful Reads:

• What is Cancer Anyway? Explaining Cancer to Children of All Ages (coloring book) by Karen L. Carney

• Because Someone I love Has Cancer: Kids Activity Book - The American Cancer Society

• When Someone You Love Has Cancer: A Guide to Help Children Cope by Alaric Lewis

• Choices in Breast Cancer Treatment: Medical Specialists and Cancer Survivors Tell You What you Need to Know by Kenneth D. Miller, MD

• Another Morning: Voices of Truth and Hope from Mothers with Cancer by Linda Blachman

• Faith, Hope and Healing: Inspiring Lessons Learned from People Living with Cancer by Bernie Siegel, MD and Jennifer Sander

• The Breast Cancer Survivor's Fitness Plan: A Doctor-Approved Workout Plan for a Strong Body and Lifesaving Results by Carolyn Kaelin, Francesca Coltrera, Jose Gardiner and Joy Prouty

References used for this publication:
• www.cancer.org
• www.webmd.com

The power of prayer:
Rely on friends and family as your warriors for healing.

QUESTIONS

41

NOTES

42

Made in United States
North Haven, CT
16 October 2023

42813043R00024